ROCK-OLOGY
The Hard Facts About Rocks

What Are Rocks Made Of?

by Ellen Lawrence

Consultants:

Shawn W. Wallace
Department of Earth and Planetary Sciences
American Museum of Natural History, New York, New York

Kimberly Brenneman, PhD
National Institute for Early Education Research, Rutgers University
New Brunswick, New Jersey

BEARPORT
PUBLISHING

New York, New York

Credits

Cover, © Kevin Eng/Shutterstock; 2–3, © Albert Russ/Shutterstock; 4, © Marcel Clemens/Shutterstock, © Kletr/Shutterstock, and © xpixel/Shutterstock; 4–5, © Pal Teravagimov/Shutterstock; 6, © Pal Teravagimov/Shutterstock; 7, © Angelina Babii/Shutterstock; 7L, © Claude Nuridsany & Marie Perennou/Science Photo Library; 8T, © Siim Sepp/Shutterstock; 8B, © Malcom Park/Superstock; 9, © Bill Perry/Shutterstock; 9R, © Alfred Pasieka/Science Photo Library; 10L, Imageman/Shutterstock; 10C, © Imageman/Shutterstock; 10R, © Weldon Schloneger/Shutterstock; 11, © Jill Reid Images/Shutterstock; 12L, © Siim Sepp/Shutterstock; 12R, © Natalia Hora/Shutterstock; 13, © Roman Samokhin/Shutterstock, © Siim Sepp/Shutterstock, © Elnur/Shutterstock, vblinov/Shutterstock, © Coprid/Shutterstock, © Vladimir Wrangel/Shutterstock, and © farbled/Shutterstock; 14, © Zev Radovan/BibleLandPictures/Alamy; 15, © Gianni Dagli Orti/The Art Archive/Alamy; 16T, © Marcel Clemens/Shutterstock; 16B, © PHOTO FUN/Shutterstock; 17, © Albert Russ/Shutterstock; 18T, © Evdokimov Maxim/Shutterstock; 18B, © PHOTO FUN/Shutterstock; 19, © Steve Vidler/Alamy; 19R, © Adrian Dennis/Corbis; 20, © blickwinkel/Hecker/Alamy; 21, © michal812/Shutterstock, © Wlad74/Shutterstock, © vvoe/Shutterstock, © Mirka Moksha/Shutterstock, © Albert Russ/Shutterstock, © Byjeng/Shutterstock, © optimarc/Shutterstock, © Gems Collection/Shutterstock, © Karol Kozlowski/Shutterstock, and © Ansis Klucis/Shutterstock; 22 L, © Africa Studio/Shutterstock; 22R, © Ruby Tuesday Books; 23TL, © Gianni Dagli Orti/The Art Archive/Alamy; 23TC, © PHOTO FUN/Shutterstock; 23TR, © Monkey Business Images/Shutterstock; 23BL, © Olga Miltsova/Shutterstock; 23BC, © yakub88/Shutterstock; 23BR, © Phil Degginger/Jack Clark Collection/Alamy.

Publisher: Kenn Goin
Editorial Director: Adam Siegel
Creative Director: Spencer Brinker
Project Editor: Natalie Lunis
Design: Elaine Wilkinson
Photo Researcher: Ruby Tuesday Books Ltd

Library of Congress Cataloging-in-Publication Data

Lawrence, Ellen, 1967– author.
  What are rocks made of? / by Ellen Lawrence.
      pages cm. — (Rock-ology)
  Audience: Ages 7–12.
  Includes bibliographical references and index.
  ISBN 978-1-62724-302-5 (library binding) — ISBN 1-62724-302-X (library binding)
  1. Rocks—Juvenile literature. 2. Petrology—Juvenile literature. I. Title. II. Title: What are rocks made of?
  QE432.2.L394 2015
  552—dc23

                          2014015806

For more information, write to Bearport Publishing Company, Inc., 45 West 21st Street, Suite 3B, New York, New York 10010. Printed in the United States of America.

10 9 8 7 6 5 4 3 2 1

Contents

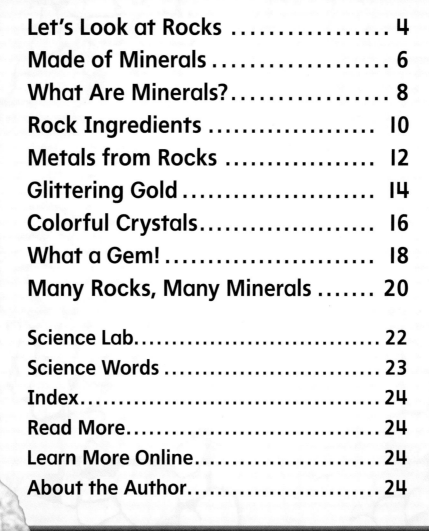

Let's Look at Rocks

There are thousands of different kinds of rocks on Earth.

They can be many different colors.

Some look dull, while others look sparkly.

Why do rocks look so different from one another?

Let's find out—what are all those rocks made of?

Made of Minerals

From a distance, the granite rock in El Capitan looks gray.

If you stand close to the rock, though, it looks speckled with black, gray, and white.

If you looked at the rock through a powerful **microscope**, you could see even more.

You would see that the rock is made of billions of tiny grains.

Each grain is made of a substance called a **mineral**.

El Capitan from a distance

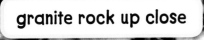

granite rock up close

granite rock seen through a powerful microscope

mineral grains

Each of the mineral grains in this picture is actually smaller than a grain of sand.

What Are Minerals?

Minerals are solid substances.

They form naturally on Earth.

Grains of minerals join together to make solid rock.

In some kinds of rock, such as granite and dolerite, the grains have straight edges.

Their shapes help the grains fit together tightly.

dolerite rock

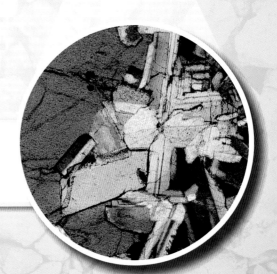

dolerite seen through a powerful microscope

sandstone
rock

In other kinds
of rock, such as
sandstone, some grains
have rounded shapes. The
larger round grains are held
together by even smaller grains.
These smaller grains act like
the cement that joins bricks
together in a brick wall.

sandstone seen
through a powerful
microscope

9

Rock Ingredients

There are more than 3,000 different minerals on Earth.

Some kinds of rocks are made of just one mineral.

Others are a mixture of several different minerals.

Granite usually contains four or five different minerals.

The two main minerals in granite are called quartz and feldspar.

chert rock

quartz

feldspar

There is lots of quartz on Earth. Many kinds of rocks contain quartz as one of their ingredients. For example, the Rainbow Rock cliffs in Oregon are made of a rock called chert that contains large amounts of quartz.

Rainbow Rock cliffs

Without rocks, we would not have metal soda cans, coins, or cars. How do you think rocks help people make these metal objects?

Metals from Rocks

Some kinds of rocks contain metal as one of their ingredients.

All metals are really minerals.

Many metals, including aluminum, copper, nickel, and silver, are removed from rocks.

Then they are made into objects that people use every day.

sandstone

Iron is a metal mineral that is removed from rocks, including sandstone, and used to make steel. Cars, buses, and trucks are all made from steel.

Below are some items made from different metals and some of the rocks in which the metals can be found.

bauxite

aluminum soda cans

copper pan

chalcopyrite

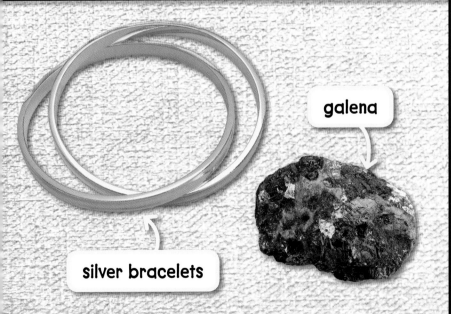

galena

silver bracelets

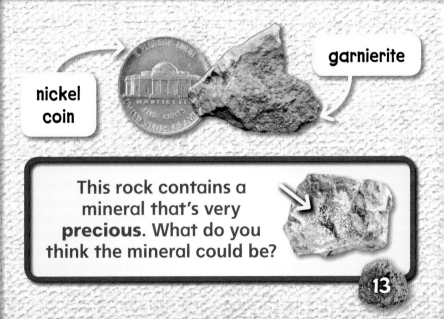

garnierite

nickel coin

This rock contains a mineral that's very **precious**. What do you think the mineral could be?

Glittering Gold

Some rocks contain tiny grains of gold.

Gold is a metal and a kind of mineral.

People first began removing gold from rock thousands of years ago.

They used it to make objects such as coins, statues, and even **coffins**.

People still use gold to make valuable jewelry today.

Gold is a **rare** mineral, which means it can be difficult to find. About 100 tons (91 metric tons) of rock are needed to find just one teaspoon of gold. That's enough rock to fill five large dump trucks!

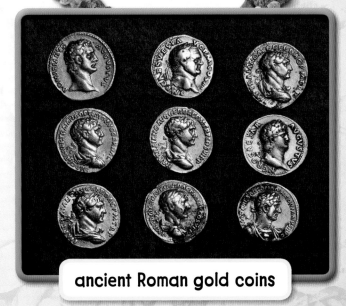

ancient Roman gold coins

This is the gold coffin of an ancient Egyptian king named Tutankhamun.

Colorful Crystals

The minerals in rocks sometimes form in shapes called **crystals**.

In some kinds of rocks, the crystals are tiny and hard to see.

In others, however, the crystals grow larger and form beautiful shapes.

Some crystals are clear, like glass, while others have pretty colors.

small green crystals in rock

clear, glasslike quartz crystals

Crystals have straight edges and smooth sides called faces.

crystal

straight edge

smooth face

Look at the crystals on these pages. How do you think people might use these beautiful-looking minerals?

17

What a Gem!

Some rocks contain mineral crystals that are especially colorful and pretty.

These crystals are removed from rocks, cut into new shapes, and polished.

Then they are used to make jewelry and valuable objects such as crowns.

Mineral crystals that are beautiful enough to be used in this way are called gemstones or gems.

Diamonds, rubies, emeralds, and sapphires are all gemstones that are found in rocks.

cutting tool

Diamonds are a super-hard mineral. They are so hard that they are used in tools that can cut through glass, rock, and metal.

tiny pieces of diamond on a cutting tool

This crown contains diamonds, rubies, emeralds, and sapphires.

Queen Elizabeth II of the United Kingdom wearing a crown

19

Many Rocks, Many Minerals

The thousands of kinds of rocks on Earth all look different.

That's because they contain different mixtures of minerals.

For example, some rocks contain lots of quartz, while others contain just a little.

Some rocks contain copper, while others contain aluminum.

From a distance, a rock may look gray and boring—but take a closer look.

It might contain colorful crystals, grains of gold, or even a precious diamond!

Many people like to collect rocks and minerals. They search for them on hillsides, cliffs, and beaches. They might also buy gemstones for their collection from special shops that sell rocks and minerals.

Minerals Chart

All the minerals shown below are found in rocks. Some are in their natural form. Others have been cut into shapes and polished to become gemstones.

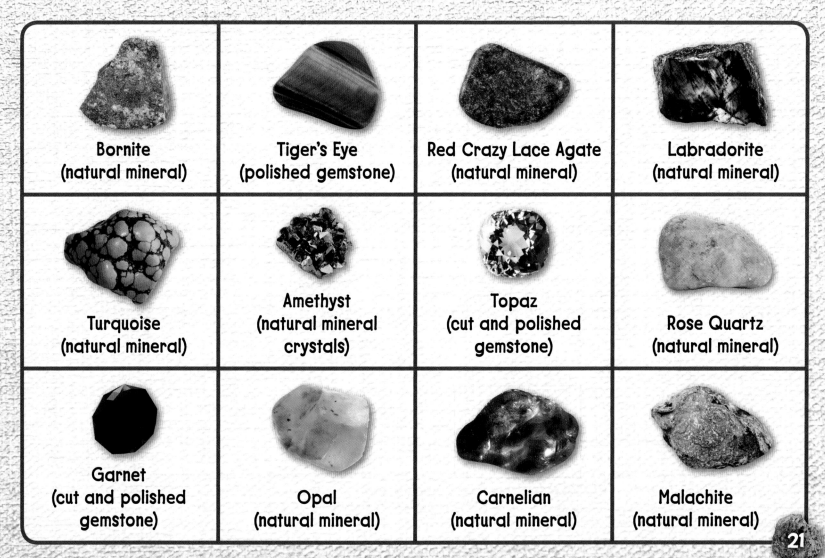

Bornite (natural mineral)	**Tiger's Eye** (polished gemstone)	**Red Crazy Lace Agate** (natural mineral)	**Labradorite** (natural mineral)
Turquoise (natural mineral)	**Amethyst** (natural mineral crystals)	**Topaz** (cut and polished gemstone)	**Rose Quartz** (natural mineral)
Garnet (cut and polished gemstone)	**Opal** (natural mineral)	**Carnelian** (natural mineral)	**Malachite** (natural mineral)

Science Lab

Mixing Minerals

Using modeling clay, pebbles, and other materials, you can show how rocks are made from different mixtures of minerals.

You will need:

- Modeling clay
- Pebbles and sand
- Beads or buttons
- Glitter

1. Begin by using different colored clay to make small rock-shaped balls.

2. Now add different mixtures of pebbles, sand, beads or buttons, and glitter to your clay rock balls.

Show your rock models to your family, friends, or teacher.

Tell them how your models are made from different ingredients. Explain how your model rocks are similar to and different from real rocks.

Science Words

coffins (KAWF-inz) containers in which bodies are placed for burial

crystals (KRISS-tuhlz) solid minerals that have formed in shapes that have straight edges and smooth sides

microscope (MYE-kruh-skohp) a tool or machine used to see things that are too small to see with the eyes alone

mineral (MIN-ur-uhl) a solid substance found in nature that makes up rocks; quartz, feldspar, and metals such as iron are all minerals

precious (PRESH-uhss) rare and very valuable; diamonds and rubies are precious gemstones

gold

rare (RAIR) not often found or seen

Index

Read More

Morganelli, Adrianna. *Minerals*. New York: Crabtree (2004).

Owen, Ruth. *Science and Craft Projects with Rocks and Soil (Get Crafty Outdoors)*. New York: PowerKids Press (2013).

Zoehfeld, Kathleen Weidner. *Rocks and Minerals*. Washington, D.C.: National Geographic (2012).

Learn More Online

To learn more about rocks and minerals, visit
www.bearportpublishing.com/Rock-ology

About the Author

Ellen Lawrence lives in the United Kingdom. Her favorite books to write are those about nature and animals. In fact, the first book Ellen bought for herself, when she was six years old, was the story of a gorilla named Patty Cake that was born in New York's Central Park Zoo.